From

Paper Routes

To

BILLIONS

By Julian Grey

Copyright © 2024 by Julian Grey.

All rights reserved. No part of this book may be reproduced, distributed, or transmitted in any form or by any means, including photocopying, recording, or other electronic or mechanical methods, without the prior written permission of the publisher, except in the case of brief quotations embodied in critical reviews and certain other noncommercial uses permitted by copyright law. This is a work of nonfiction Names, characters, places, imagination or used fictitiously. Any resemblance to actual persons, living or dead, or actual events is purely coincidental.

PRINTED IN THE UNITED STATES OF AMERICA

Contents

Introduction 3

Humble Beginnings – The Making of a Young Entrepreneur 12

The Education of a Financial Genius 25

Building the Buffett Empire – Berkshire Hathaway Begins 37

The Buffett Way – Five Strategies That Made Him Great 49

Wisdom from the Oracle of Omaha 59

Warren Buffett's Greatest Investments 69

Buffett the Teacher – Lessons for Life and Business 79

The Legacy of Warren Buffett – The Billionaire Who Inspired the World. 88

Introduction

From Paper Routes to Billions

"The best investment you can make is in yourself." – Warren Buffett

Warren Buffett's journey is unlike any other—a story of extraordinary vision, patience, and an unwavering commitment to principles. A child of the Great Depression, Buffett rose from humble beginnings in Omaha, Nebraska, to become one of the world's richest and most respected individuals. Yet, his wealth is not his only legacy; it's the philosophy he championed—simple, powerful principles that anyone can apply to transform their financial life.

At the heart of Buffett's story is a lesson: success does not come from luck, connections, or shortcuts. It comes from timeless habits, consistent strategies, and the ability to think differently when others are chasing fads. Buffett's rise to prominence was not overnight; it was the result of years of compounding, discipline, and a relentless focus on value. His life shows that wealth is not reserved for the elite—it is attainable for anyone who is willing to learn, think long-term, and put in the effort.

But this book is about more than Warren Buffett's billions. It's about how his five powerful wealth-building strategies can help *you* achieve financial security, confidence, and freedom. Whether you are an aspiring investor, a small business owner, or someone simply looking to improve your financial future, Buffett's story will inspire you to take control of your money and your life.

The Early Spark – A Boy Who Loved Numbers

Warren Edward Buffett was born on August 30, 1930, in Omaha, Nebraska, to a modest but hardworking family. His father, Howard Buffett, was a stockbroker and a congressman, while his mother, Leila Buffett, focused on raising their three children. Growing up during the Great Depression, Warren witnessed the value of every single dollar. Times were tough for many families in America, and these formative years instilled in him a respect for money that would guide his life's path.

Unlike other children his age, Warren found joy not in toys or games but in numbers. At a young age, he would spend hours reading books on business and finance that most adults would struggle to comprehend. When other kids were dreaming of becoming astronauts or firefighters, Warren was fascinated by ways to make money—and to make it grow.

The defining moment came when he stumbled across a book at the local library titled *"One Thousand Ways to Make $1,000."* For Warren, this was not just a book—it was a blueprint. The idea of compounding small sums into larger ones captivated him. He realized that money, when invested wisely, could do the heavy lifting for you. This idea planted a seed in his mind that would later blossom into his legendary investment philosophy.

A Born Entrepreneur

Buffett's entrepreneurial instincts emerged early. By the age of 6, he was buying packs of gum and bottles of Coca-Cola from his grandfather's grocery store and selling them to neighbors at a profit. This was his first taste of the thrill of business—of turning a small investment into real returns.

At age 11, Buffett made his first stock market investment. Using money he had earned from his paper route, he bought three shares of Cities Service Preferred stock at $38 per share. Soon after, the stock price fell to $27, and young Warren faced his first investor's dilemma: hold on or sell in panic. True to his growing instincts, he held on until the stock rebounded to $40. He sold for a small profit, only to watch the stock soar to $200 shortly afterward. It was a lesson he would never forget: patience pays, and hasty decisions often cost more in the long run.

By high school, Buffett was earning more than some adults. His paper route and other small ventures—such as pinball machine businesses—made him thousands of dollars, an extraordinary feat for a teenager. He even filed his first tax return at age 14, proudly deducting the cost of his bicycle as a business expense.

These experiences were more than childhood hustles; they were the foundation of Buffett's belief in *taking action* and *seizing opportunities.* He learned that building wealth was not about making a single lucky bet—it was about consistently making smart decisions, no matter how small.

The Buffett Difference – Thinking Long-Term

What set Warren Buffett apart, even as a young man, was his ability to think long-term. While most people chased instant gratification, Buffett understood the power of delayed rewards. He saw money not just as currency but as a tool that could grow exponentially if given time.

This perspective would later become a cornerstone of his investing philosophy. Buffett's mantra, "Our favorite holding period is forever," highlights his belief in buying undervalued businesses and holding them for the long haul. He understood that true wealth is built not through quick flips but through steady compounding over decades.

But Buffett's success is not just about numbers or stocks. It's about the mindset behind his actions—the ability to remain calm when others panic, to think independently, and to focus on long-term value rather than short-term noise. These are the principles that enabled him to turn small, humble beginnings into a global empire.

What You Will Learn from This Book

The purpose of this book is simple: to make Warren Buffett's strategies accessible to you. This is not a book about becoming a billionaire overnight. Instead, it's a guide to thinking, investing, and living like Warren Buffett—habits that can transform your financial future, no matter where you start.

By studying Buffett's life and his five wealth-building strategies, you will learn:

1. **How to Think Like an Investor** – Master the principles of value investing and learn to spot opportunities others miss.

2. **The Power of Patience** – Discover why holding investments for the long-term creates life-changing wealth.

3. **How to Harness Compound Growth** – Understand the magic of compounding and how it can work for you.

4. **Why Simplicity Beats Complexity** – Learn how Buffett avoids hype and focuses on fundamentals to make smarter decisions.

5. **How to Apply Buffett's Wisdom in Your Own Life** – Practical, actionable strategies to grow your wealth and achieve financial freedom.

Buffett's story is proof that success is not reserved for the privileged. He did not come from wealth. He did not rely on luck. Instead, he focused on learning, discipline, and consistency. By applying these same principles, you too can achieve extraordinary results.

A Timeless Legacy

Warren Buffett is more than an investor; he is a teacher. Through his annual letters, speeches, and example, he has shared the secrets to his success with anyone willing to listen. This book is your opportunity to learn from the best.

Buffett's life shows that building wealth is not about having a high-paying job or inheriting money. It's about making smart decisions, living below your means, and letting time work in your favor. As Buffett himself once said, *"The chains of habit are too light to be felt until they are too heavy to be broken."* The habits you build today—whether in saving, investing, or thinking—will determine your future.

This is the story of a boy with a paper route who became the Oracle of Omaha. But more importantly, it's a story of timeless principles that anyone can follow.

Are you ready to learn from the world's greatest investor? Are you ready to take control of your financial future and build a legacy of your own?

Let's begin.

Chapter 1:
Humble Beginnings – The Making of a Young Entrepreneur

Warren Buffett, known today as the "Oracle of Omaha," has become a household name synonymous with wealth, wisdom, and investing brilliance. But long before he amassed his billions, Buffett was an ordinary boy from a small Midwestern town, shaped by humble beginnings and an unquenchable curiosity about money and numbers. His story is not one of privilege but of perseverance, practicality, and a relentless drive to understand how money works.

Buffett's journey began at a time when America was reeling from the economic devastation of the Great Depression. The challenges of those early years—combined with his family's strong moral compass and his innate entrepreneurial spirit—laid the foundation for a future that no one could have predicted.

For those seeking to learn from Buffett's extraordinary rise, this chapter reveals the building blocks of his character and success. It demonstrates how an early focus on discipline, frugality, and opportunity—lessons any reader can apply—can be the catalyst for a life of achievement.

The Early Years in Omaha

Warren Edward Buffett was born on **August 30, 1930**, in Omaha, Nebraska. This unassuming Midwestern city, surrounded by cornfields and wide-open plains, was far removed from the bustling financial hubs of New York or Chicago. Yet, Omaha would forever remain Buffett's home, both physically and spiritually, symbolizing the values of simplicity and stability that would guide his life.

Buffett's arrival into the world came during one of the most turbulent times in American history: the Great Depression. The economic collapse of 1929 shattered millions of lives, wiping out savings, jobs, and opportunities. Families across the nation—including the Buffets—had to learn to survive on less, often stretching every dollar as far as it could go.

The Great Depression shaped young Warren's financial mindset in profound ways. He grew up hearing stories of families losing everything they owned and witnessed firsthand how hard people worked to make ends meet. These lessons were not abstract for him—they were part of his everyday life. Frugality became second nature, and he understood early that money was not something to be wasted but something to be respected and grown.

Buffett's father, **Howard Buffett**, played an instrumental role in shaping Warren's values. Howard was a stockbroker by trade, which gave Warren his first exposure to the world of finance. However, Howard was more than a businessman; he was also a man of deep ethics, faith, and unwavering principles. Later in life, Howard served multiple terms as a Republican congressman, known for his integrity and strong stance on personal responsibility.

Warren learned two crucial lessons from his father that would follow him for the rest of his life:

1. **Ethics matter more than money.** Warren saw firsthand that trust and integrity were invaluable currencies. Howard's refusal to compromise his principles—even during tough financial times—left a lasting impression on his son.

2. **Financial discipline is key to survival.** Howard often discussed the importance of saving, investing, and living within one's means. This mindset—paired with the hardships of the Depression—helped Warren develop a respect for

money that would define his future decisions.

These early years gave Buffett something priceless: the understanding that financial success was not about luck but about making wise decisions, avoiding waste, and embracing long-term thinking.

Signs of a Budding Businessman

Warren Buffett's entrepreneurial instincts began to surface at an early age. While most children were content with playing games or toys, Warren found excitement in making money—no matter how small the sums. Even as a young boy, he was driven not by greed but by the thrill of building something of value.

At the age of **six**, Warren made his first recorded profit. He purchased a pack of gum from his grandfather's grocery store for a nickel and sold individual sticks to neighbors at a slight markup. Soon after, he moved on to bigger ventures, like selling **Coca-Cola bottles** door to door. Buying six-packs of Coke for 25 cents, he would sell each bottle for a nickel, turning a 5-cent profit on each pack. For Warren, the math was simple: small profits added up, and every opportunity to sell something was an opportunity to grow his "business."

These small hustles were not just about making pocket money—they were a reflection of Buffett's ability to spot value where others saw none. He understood, even then, the basics of **buying low and selling high**, a skill that would later make him one of the greatest investors of all time.

By the time Warren reached his early teens, his entrepreneurial ventures were generating real income. His most successful childhood hustle came from delivering **newspapers**. At the time, paper routes were a common way for boys to earn extra money, but Warren approached it differently. Instead of treating it as a chore, he treated it as a business.

Warren optimized his route, managed subscriptions efficiently, and saved every penny he earned. By age 14, his paper route and other ventures had earned him **$1,200**—the equivalent of over $20,000 in today's money. This was an astonishing achievement for a teenager in the 1940s.

Rather than spending his earnings on toys or luxuries, Warren made his first big financial decision: he used $1,200 to buy **40 acres of farmland** in Nebraska. He leased the land to local farmers, who worked the property while he earned steady rental income. This early investment taught Warren a critical lesson:

Assets can work for you, even when you're not working yourself.

This realization—that money invested wisely can create passive income—became a cornerstone of Buffett's philosophy.

At **age 11**, Warren made his first foray into the **stock market**, an experience that would shape his career forever. Using money he had saved; he purchased three shares of **Cities Service Preferred** stock at $38 per share. The stock price quickly dropped to $27, testing Warren's resolve. Despite the temptation to cut his losses, Warren held on until the stock rebounded to $40, at which point he sold his shares for a small profit.

However, the story didn't end there. Shortly after Warren sold, the stock skyrocketed to $200 per share. This experience gave Warren two invaluable lessons:

1. **Patience is key to success in investing.** Hasty decisions can cost more than temporary losses.

2. **Emotions can be dangerous in the stock market.** Staying calm and sticking to a plan often pays off in the long run.

For most children, these experiences would have been little more than passing anecdotes. But for Warren Buffett, they were the building blocks of a lifelong career. He was learning lessons about **risk, reward, patience, and value** long before most adults even considered such concepts.

A Lifelong Love for Numbers

While Warren Buffett had a clear knack for business, his true passion was for **numbers**. He was fascinated by their power to tell stories, reveal opportunities, and unlock wealth.

As a boy, Warren spent countless hours reading books that most children would never even consider. One of the most influential books he encountered was **"One Thousand Ways to Make $1,000."** Written in the early 20th century, the book was a practical guide to small-business ideas and entrepreneurial ventures. But for Warren, it was more than a book—it was a revelation.

The book introduced Warren to the concept of **compounding**—the idea that small sums of money, invested wisely, could grow exponentially over time. To young Warren, this idea was like discovering a secret formula for wealth. Compounding became a lifelong obsession, one that would later define his investing strategy and help him build his fortune.

To illustrate, Warren often shared the example of a snowball rolling down a hill. If you start small but let the snowball roll long enough, it will grow larger and larger on its own. Similarly, small investments can grow into massive sums if given enough time. This lesson—that time and consistency are your greatest allies—became a key part of Buffett's philosophy.

Buffett's love for numbers extended beyond books. He enjoyed analyzing **balance sheets, financial reports, and stock prices**—even as a teenager. Where others saw boring data, Warren saw opportunities. He developed an uncanny ability to spot value hidden in the numbers, a skill that would later make him a world-class investor.

Buffett's analytical mind set him apart. He understood that success in business and investing wasn't about luck—it was about understanding the numbers, finding undervalued opportunities, and letting time do its work. This is a lesson anyone can apply. Whether you're starting a small business, saving for retirement, or looking to invest, the ability to think in terms of numbers—and to trust the math—can be your greatest advantage.

Practical Takeaways from Buffett's Humble Beginnings

Warren Buffett's early years offer lessons that are as relevant today as they were decades ago:

1. **Start Early**

    Buffett began saving, investing, and building businesses as a child. The earlier you start, the greater the power of compounding can work in your favor.

2. **Value Hard Work and Discipline**

    Buffett learned the importance of discipline from his paper routes and entrepreneurial ventures. Success rarely comes overnight—it comes from consistency and persistence.

3. **Invest in Assets**

    Buffett's farmland investment taught him that assets can generate income even when you're not working. Look for opportunities to build passive income streams.

4. **Think Long-Term**

    Buffett's early experience in the stock market taught him the value of patience. Avoid chasing quick wins and focus on long-term rewards.

5. **Respect Money**

    - Growing up during the Depression taught Buffett to

treat money with respect. Frugality, saving, and living within your means are timeless principles.

Chapter 2:

The Education of a Financial Genius

Warren Buffett's journey to becoming one of the world's most brilliant financial minds was not just a product of innate talent. It was forged through years of education, mentorship, and a relentless thirst for knowledge. While his childhood set the foundation for his entrepreneurial instincts, it was his formal education and exposure to great thinkers that refined his approach to investing and solidified his legendary strategies.

Unlike many, Buffett was never content with surface-level understanding. He approached education the way he approached investing: with discipline, focus, and a belief in long-term rewards. This chapter explores how Buffett's intellectual journey—from classrooms in Nebraska to prestigious halls at Columbia Business School—shaped his principles, introduced him to life-changing mentors, and taught him to see the financial world in a way no one else could.

Learning from the Greats

Warren Buffett's educational path began in Omaha, but it would soon take him to institutions where he would encounter life-altering ideas and mentors. After graduating high school at **age 16**, Buffett enrolled at the **University of Pennsylvania**. He initially attended the Wharton School but transferred back home to finish his degree at the **University of Nebraska**, where tuition was cheaper—a classic Buffett move that reflected his respect for value.

Buffett's time at the University of Nebraska was significant not because of the school itself, but because of his unrelenting curiosity. While other students were content to fulfill basic coursework, Buffett consumed knowledge voraciously. He read books, newspapers, and financial reports—anything that would expand his understanding of business and investing. Even at a young age, Warren believed that education wasn't about getting a degree; it was about acquiring tools to succeed in the real world.

At Nebraska, Buffett's brilliance began to shine. He completed his undergraduate degree in just **three years**, graduating at the top of his class. Yet, Warren knew that true success required learning from those who had already mastered their fields.

After reading a book that would change his life—**"The Intelligent Investor"** by **Benjamin Graham**—Buffett decided to apply to **Columbia Business School**. Graham, widely regarded as the father of value investing, was a professor there. Buffett's decision was driven not by prestige or career prospects, but by a single goal: to learn directly from a master.

At Columbia, Warren found exactly what he was looking for. Benjamin Graham's teachings were unlike anything Buffett had ever encountered. Graham emphasized that stocks were not just numbers on a ticker—they represented real businesses with real value. This idea transformed how Warren viewed investing.

Under Graham, Buffett learned three core principles that would define his future success:

1. **Value Over Price:** Graham taught that a stock's price often has little to do with its actual worth. Investors should focus on intrinsic value—the true measure of a company's health and potential.

2. **Margin of Safety:** Investors should only buy stocks when they are priced well below their intrinsic value, ensuring a

buffer against mistakes or market volatility.

3. **Emotional Discipline:** Graham believed the greatest threat to an investor's success was not the market, but their own emotions. Buffett would later describe this as the need to "be greedy when others are fearful and fearful when others are greedy."

Warren didn't just learn from Graham—he absorbed his philosophy like a sponge. Graham became more than a teacher; he became Buffett's mentor, shaping how Warren approached every investment decision for the rest of his life.

In later years, Buffett often spoke of Graham's profound influence, calling him "the second most important person in my life after my father."

The Power of "Margin of Safety"

One of the most transformative ideas Buffett learned from Benjamin Graham was the concept of **"margin of safety"**. To Graham, and subsequently to Buffett, this was more than a rule—it was an investment philosophy.

The "margin of safety" principle is simple but powerful: when purchasing a stock, you must ensure that the price you pay is significantly below its intrinsic value. This creates a "safety cushion" in case your analysis is incorrect or unexpected events cause the stock's value to drop.

To illustrate, Buffett often compared the margin of safety to building a bridge. If an engineer designs a bridge to support 10,000 pounds, they don't stop there—they build the bridge to withstand 15,000 pounds to ensure it's safe. Similarly, when investing, buying stocks far below their intrinsic value provides protection against bad decisions or market downturns.

Buffett would later use this principle to make some of the most successful investments in history. By focusing on undervalued companies, he ensured that his money worked efficiently while minimizing risk.

However, Warren's genius lay not just in understanding Graham's teachings but in adapting them. While Graham focused primarily on **quantitative factors** (like balance sheets and financial ratios), Buffett saw the potential to include **qualitative factors**—such as a company's brand, management, and competitive advantage. This blend of art and science would set Buffett apart from other investors.

In one of his early interviews, Buffett described the concept eloquently:

"The stock market is filled with individuals who know the price of everything, but the value of nothing."

By focusing on value and demanding a margin of safety, Buffett learned to separate himself from the noise of the market. This principle remains one of the most important lessons for any aspiring investor: always buy value, never buy hype.

Finding His Path

Warren Buffett's education extended far beyond the classroom. After graduating from Columbia, he was determined to work for his mentor Benjamin Graham. Buffett applied to Graham's investment firm, Graham-Newman Corporation, but was initially rejected. Undeterred, Warren returned to Omaha and took on various financial jobs, including working at his father's brokerage firm.

These years were not glamorous, but they were pivotal. Buffett spent countless hours reading financial reports, analyzing companies, and building his skills. His days were marked by discipline and his nights by endless study. Warren knew that success would not come quickly, but he trusted that his dedication to learning and value investing would eventually pay off.

Buffett's persistence soon caught the attention of Graham. In **1954**, Graham offered Warren a job at Graham-Newman. For Buffett, this was a dream come true—a chance to learn directly from the man he admired most.

Working for Graham was like earning a Ph.D. in investing. Buffett spent his days analyzing undervalued stocks, applying Graham's methods, and refining his own approach. During this time, Warren began to understand the importance of patience and long-term thinking. Graham taught him that success in investing was not about chasing quick profits but about identifying opportunities and waiting for them to grow.

While Buffett loved his time at Graham-Newman, he began to see limitations in Graham's approach. Graham's method was purely mathematical—focused solely on numbers and undervaluation. But Buffett believed there was more to investing. He began to develop his own philosophy, combining Graham's principles with his belief in the importance of high-quality companies.

In **1956**, Graham retired, and Warren Buffett made a bold decision. He returned to Omaha, determined to start his own investment partnership. By this point, Buffett had everything he needed: the principles of value investing, the lessons of margin of safety, and the discipline to follow his passion full-time.

The decision to strike out on his own was not without risk, but Buffett knew one thing for certain:

True success comes from doing what you love, and doing it with conviction.

Practical Takeaways from Buffett's Education

Warren Buffett's journey as a student and protégé offers practical lessons for anyone seeking success:

1. **Seek Out Mentors**

    Surround yourself with people who are smarter and more experienced than you. Buffett's success would not have been possible without Benjamin Graham.

2. **Focus on Value, Not Hype**

    Always ask, "What is this worth?" rather than, "What is its price?" Buffett's ability to see value where others could not became his greatest asset.

3. **Embrace the Margin of Safety**

    Protect yourself against risks by ensuring you always buy assets at a significant discount to their intrinsic value.

4. **Never Stop Learning**

    Buffett's education did not end in the classroom. His relentless pursuit of knowledge set him apart.

5. **Follow Your Passion**

    Buffett chose to pursue investing full-time, even when it meant taking risks. His love for his work fueled his success.

Chapter 3:

Building the Buffett Empire – Berkshire Hathaway Begins

Warren Buffett's rise from a promising investor to the architect of one of the most influential companies in history was a journey marked by bold decisions, unexpected lessons, and unparalleled vision. At the heart of his empire lies **Berkshire Hathaway**, a name synonymous with Buffett's genius and long-term investment strategy. However, the road to Berkshire's success was not straightforward; it began as what Buffett himself described as a **"colossal mistake"** and turned into one of the greatest business transformations ever seen.

This chapter explores the origins of Berkshire Hathaway, Buffett's commitment to **value investing**, and the strategic moves that turned the struggling textile company into a globally renowned conglomerate.

The Takeover of Berkshire Hathaway

Warren Buffett's relationship with Berkshire Hathaway began not as a calculated move, but as an emotional reaction. In the early 1960s, Berkshire Hathaway was a failing textile company based in New England. Its outdated mills and declining competitiveness made it a textbook case of an industry headed for extinction. Buffett first noticed Berkshire in **1962** when its stock price appeared undervalued relative to its assets. True to his value-investing philosophy, he began buying shares at an average price of **$7.50** per share.

Buffett viewed Berkshire as a classic "**cigar butt**" investment—a term borrowed from Benjamin Graham. Just like picking up an old cigar on the sidewalk for one last puff, these companies had little future but offered a short-term gain if purchased cheaply enough.

What happened next became legendary in Buffett's career. In **1964**, the management of Berkshire Hathaway, led by CEO Seabury Stanton, made Buffett an offer to buy back his shares at **$11.50**. Buffett agreed, but when he received the formal tender offer, the price had been lowered to **$11.375** per share. Feeling cheated, Buffett responded not with anger, but with action. He bought enough shares to take control of the company and fired Stanton.

Years later, Buffett would reflect on this decision with candor, calling it a mistake:

"If you're emotional about investment, you're not going to do well. You can't get attached to a stock."

At the time, Berkshire Hathaway was losing money and had little chance of revival as a textile business. Buffett soon realized that running a struggling textile company was a far cry from his core passion: investing in undervalued assets. However, instead of abandoning Berkshire, Buffett turned the situation into an opportunity.

This episode marked an essential lesson: mistakes in business are inevitable, but what matters is how you adapt and move forward. Buffett's response to this mistake ultimately paved the way for the creation of a new kind of business empire.

The Principles of Value Investing

While Buffett's initial purchase of Berkshire Hathaway was emotionally driven, his ability to salvage and transform the company was guided by his unwavering commitment to **value investing**. Buffett believed in identifying companies whose stock prices were undervalued compared to their **intrinsic value**—a principle instilled in him by Benjamin Graham.

Rather than throwing good money after bad in the textile business, Buffett decided to leverage Berkshire as an investment vehicle. He began channeling the company's cash flow into purchasing stocks of businesses that met his strict investment criteria:

1. **Strong, Sustainable Earnings** – Buffett sought companies with proven earnings power and predictable future performance.

2. **Great Management** – He believed in backing companies with honest, capable leaders.

3. **Competitive Moats** – Buffett focused on businesses with durable competitive advantages that could protect them from rivals.

4. **Undervalued Price** – Above all, the price had to be far below the company's intrinsic value, ensuring a margin of safety.

With these principles in mind, Buffett made his first strategic acquisitions under the Berkshire Hathaway banner. Some of his early investments were modest but highly profitable. Notable examples included:

- **American Express (1964):** After the "salad oil scandal" caused the company's stock to plummet, Buffett saw an opportunity. He believed in the strength of the American Express brand and invested heavily. The decision paid off as the company rebounded and delivered massive returns.

- **The Washington Post (1973):** Buffett purchased shares in the struggling newspaper company when others shied away. His belief in its management and long-term value proved correct, turning it into a highly successful investment.

- **GEICO (1976):** Buffett's fascination with GEICO dated back to his days studying under Benjamin Graham.

When the company hit hard times, Buffett invested $45 million, recognizing its powerful business model and potential for recovery.

Each of these investments showcased Buffett's unique ability to see opportunities where others saw failure. He demonstrated that value investing was not about following the crowd but about having the patience and discipline to act when others were fearful.

Transitioning to a Holding Company

By the late 1960s, Buffett recognized that Berkshire Hathaway's textile operations were a lost cause. Rather than clinging to a dying industry, he made a critical decision: **transforming Berkshire Hathaway into a diversified holding company.**

Buffett began acquiring businesses outright, focusing on industries that offered consistent earnings and long-term growth. Unlike traditional conglomerates that often overpaid for acquisitions, Buffett stuck to his value principles. He purchased companies with strong fundamentals, capable management, and durable competitive advantages.

One of the first businesses Buffett acquired under this new model was **National Indemnity Company**, a small but profitable insurance firm. The move was significant because it introduced Buffett to the power of the **insurance float.**

In insurance, companies collect premiums upfront and pay claims later, creating a pool of money known as the float. Buffett realized that he could invest this float to generate additional returns—a strategy that would become the cornerstone of Berkshire Hathaway's success.

Over time, Buffett used Berkshire's growing float to fund more acquisitions and investments. This compounding effect allowed him to transform Berkshire into a powerhouse conglomerate. By reinvesting profits into high-quality businesses, Buffett created a snowball effect, where returns built upon returns year after year.

Key acquisitions during this period included:

- **See's Candies (1972):** Buffett paid $25 million for this premium chocolate company, a price many believed was too high. However, See's had a loyal customer base and consistent cash flow, making it a perfect fit for Berkshire's portfolio.

- **Buffalo Evening News (1977):** Buffett saw an opportunity to acquire a struggling newspaper and turn it around with smart management.

- **Nebraska Furniture Mart (1983):** Buffett admired the company's founder, Rose Blumkin, for her business acumen and relentless work ethic. The acquisition reinforced Buffett's belief in backing strong leaders.

Each of these businesses shared a common thread: they were simple, profitable, and built to last. Buffett's ability to identify these opportunities—and his commitment to letting great companies run with minimal interference—set him apart as a business leader.

By the 1980s, Berkshire Hathaway had evolved into more than just a holding company. It became a symbol of Buffett's philosophy: focus on long-term value, avoid unnecessary risks, and let compounding work its magic.

Practical Takeaways from Building the Empire

Warren Buffett's transformation of Berkshire Hathaway offers timeless lessons for aspiring entrepreneurs and investors:

1. **Learn from Your Mistakes**

    Buffett turned his emotional decision into a life-changing opportunity. Mistakes are inevitable, but resilience and adaptation are key to long-term success.

2. **Stick to Your Principles**

    Buffett's unwavering commitment to value investing allowed him to see opportunities others missed.

3. **Invest in What You Understand**

    Buffett avoided complicated businesses and focused on simple, profitable companies with strong fundamentals.

4. **Embrace Long-Term Thinking**

    The power of compounding works best when you have patience. Buffett built Berkshire's empire slowly but steadily, always focusing on the future.

5. **Reinvest Profits Wisely**

    Buffett's use of insurance float to fund acquisitions highlights the importance of reinvesting cash flow to fuel growth.

Chapter 4:

The Buffett Way – Five Strategies That Made Him Great

Warren Buffett's legendary success is not the result of complex formulas or secret shortcuts. Instead, it is grounded in **five timeless strategies** that anyone can understand and apply. Buffett's approach to investing, often referred to as "The Buffett Way," has made him not only one of the richest individuals in the world but also a beacon of wisdom for investors of all levels.

In this chapter, we'll explore the key strategies that have defined Buffett's career: his commitment to **long-term thinking**, his focus on **value over hype**, and his mastery of the **power of compound interest**. Through real-life case studies and practical insights, we'll uncover how these principles have transformed

Buffett's investments into billions—and how they can guide you toward financial success.

The Art of Long-Term Thinking

One of Warren Buffett's most enduring principles is his belief in **long-term investing**. While many investors chase short-term gains, Buffett plays the long game, often holding onto stocks for **decades**. His philosophy is simple:

"The stock market is a device for transferring money from the impatient to the patient."

Buffett's approach is rooted in the idea that **great businesses grow in value over time**. By investing in companies with strong fundamentals and holding onto them, investors can reap the rewards of compounding growth, consistent dividends, and increased share value.

Case Study: Coca-Cola – A Masterclass in Long-Term Investing

In **1988**, Buffett made a bold investment in Coca-Cola, purchasing $1 billion worth of shares. At the time, Coca-Cola was already a well-established global brand, but its stock price was undervalued. Buffett saw an opportunity. He believed in Coca-Cola's strong market position, brand loyalty, and ability to generate consistent profits.

Fast forward to today: Buffett's investment in Coca-Cola has grown **over 20 times in value**, and Berkshire Hathaway receives hundreds of millions in dividends annually. Coca-Cola remains a cornerstone of Berkshire's portfolio, demonstrating the power of Buffett's long-term thinking.

Other Long-Term Wins

- **American Express:** Buffett invested in the company during the 1960s when it faced a temporary crisis. His long-term faith in American Express's brand and business model turned the investment into a massive success.

- **Apple:** In recent years, Buffett's bet on Apple showcased his adaptability and long-term vision. Despite entering the tech sector cautiously, Buffett recognized Apple's ability to generate consistent cash flow and build customer loyalty. Today, it is one of Berkshire Hathaway's most significant holdings.

Takeaway: Patience Pays Off

Buffett teaches us that successful investing is not about timing the market but about **time in the market**. Instead of trading stocks frequently, focus on identifying great businesses, investing for the long term, and letting the value compound over time.

Value Over Hype

In an era where many investors are drawn to flashy trends, Buffett's strategy stands as a counterpoint. He firmly avoids **hyped investments** and sticks to businesses that offer real, measurable value. Buffett's decisions are guided by numbers, not narratives. He often quips:

"Beware the investment activity that produces applause; the great moves are usually greeted by yawns."

Why Buffett Avoids Trends

Hype-driven investments often lack solid fundamentals. Whether it's the dot-com bubble of the late 1990s or speculative cryptocurrencies in recent years, Buffett steers clear of assets that are driven by excitement rather than economic performance. For him, the value of a company comes from its ability to generate real profits, maintain competitive advantages, and withstand market cycles.

Case Study: The Dot-Com Bubble

In the late 1990s, technology stocks were all the rage. Investors poured billions into unprofitable startups, hoping to ride the wave of innovation. Many questioned Buffett's decision to stay on the sidelines, accusing him of being "out of touch." However, Buffett knew that most of these companies lacked sustainable business models.

When the bubble burst in **2000**, tech stocks collapsed, wiping out trillions of dollars in market value. Buffett's refusal to chase the hype protected Berkshire Hathaway's capital and allowed him to invest in undervalued opportunities after the crash.

The Importance of Fundamentals

Buffett's approach teaches us to focus on businesses that:

1. Generate consistent **profits and cash flow.**
2. Have a clear **competitive advantage** (or economic moat).
3. Are priced below their intrinsic value.

By ignoring hype and focusing on these fundamentals, investors can avoid costly mistakes and build a portfolio of solid, long-term winners.

Takeaway: Ignore the Noise

The lesson from Buffett is clear: avoid fads, speculation, and "too-good-to-be-true" opportunities. True wealth comes from investing in businesses with lasting value.

The Power of Compound Interest

If there's one principle that Warren Buffett considers the cornerstone of wealth-building, it's **compound interest**. Often referred to as the "eighth wonder of the world," compounding allows money to grow exponentially over time by reinvesting earnings.

Buffett is a living example of the power of compounding. By starting early, reinvesting his profits, and allowing his investments to grow for decades, Buffett turned modest sums into billions.

The Simple Math of Compounding

Here's how compounding works in its simplest form:

- Suppose you invest **$1,000** at an annual return of **10%**.

- At the end of the first year, your investment grows to **$1,100**.

- Instead of withdrawing the $100 profit, you reinvest it. In year two, you earn **10%** on $1,100, growing your total to **$1,210**.

- Over time, this process accelerates. By year 20, your initial $1,000 grows to **$6,727**—without adding another dollar!

Buffett emphasizes that compounding works best when paired with **time and patience**. The earlier you start investing, the greater the impact of compounding.

Real-Life Example: Buffett's Investment Timeline

- At age **11**, Buffett made his first stock purchase, buying three shares of Cities Service Preferred.
- By age **30**, his net worth was around **$1 million**.
- By age **50**, it had grown to **$300 million**.
- Today, over **90% of Buffett's wealth** was accumulated after he turned **65**.

The takeaway? Compounding doesn't happen overnight. The secret is to start early, reinvest earnings, and let time do the heavy lifting.

How You Can Apply Compounding

1. **Start Investing Early:** The earlier you begin, the longer your money has to compound.
2. **Reinvest Your Profits:** Whether it's dividends, interest, or capital gains, reinvest your earnings to fuel exponential growth.

3. **Be Patient:** Avoid withdrawing money prematurely. Compounding rewards those who let their investments grow over time.

Practical Takeaways from Buffett's Strategies

Warren Buffett's success is built on principles that are accessible to everyone:

1. **Think Long Term:** Hold great businesses for decades, not months.
2. **Focus on Value:** Invest based on fundamentals, not hype or trends.
3. **Harness Compounding:** Allow time and reinvestment to multiply your returns.

Buffett's strategies are not about chasing the next big thing. Instead, they emphasize **discipline, patience, and consistency**— qualities that any investor can develop.

Chapter 5:
Wisdom from the Oracle of Omaha

Warren Buffett, often referred to as the "Oracle of Omaha," is celebrated not only for his business acumen but for his deeply rooted wisdom. Throughout his decades-long career, he has consistently shared valuable life lessons—principles that extend far beyond investing. The core of his success lies in a few key ideas that anyone can adopt, no matter their stage in life or financial journey. In this chapter, we will explore the three pillars of Buffett's wisdom: the **power of patience and discipline**, the **importance of integrity and reputation**, and how to **think like Warren Buffett** in order to make better decisions and grow both financially and personally.

The Power of Patience and Discipline

Buffett's success is not built on quick decisions or rapid financial maneuvers. Instead, it is the product of **patience** and **discipline**. For Buffett, **delayed gratification** is essential—not just in investing but in life. He once said:

"The stock market is a device for transferring money from the impatient to the patient."

Patience is a cornerstone of Buffett's investing philosophy. He has always adhered to the belief that great companies should be held for **decades**, allowing their value to grow, rather than trading them for short-term gains. His strategy encourages investors to **wait for the right opportunities** and to resist the urge to make hasty decisions based on market noise or external pressure.

Delayed Gratification in Investing

Buffett's investment style involves buying companies at attractive prices and holding them for the long term. He often states that his favorite holding period is "**forever.**" This commitment to long-term success is deeply ingrained in his approach to investing. The idea is simple: buy when others are fearful, and hold for long-term growth.

Consider his **investment in See's Candies**: In the 1970s, Buffett purchased See's Candies for $25 million. Over the years, See's has generated **billions** in profits for Berkshire Hathaway. But what makes this investment even more remarkable is Buffett's refusal to sell the business—even when offered enormous sums of money. His patience, in this case, paid off handsomely.

Patience Beyond Investing

Patience is not just for the stock market. Buffett also applies this principle in his personal life. He avoids impulsive decisions, whether in business or relationships. His wisdom teaches us that some of the best opportunities require time to mature. It's a lesson that, when applied in life, can reduce stress, increase success, and bring lasting happiness.

Takeaway: Slow and Steady Wins the Race

To build wealth—and to live a fulfilled life—patience is key. Buffett teaches us that we shouldn't expect quick results, but instead focus on consistency, discipline, and a long-term perspective. By mastering patience, you allow yourself the space to make wiser, more deliberate decisions.

The Importance of Integrity and Reputation

For Buffett, **integrity** and **reputation** are among the most important assets an individual can possess. He often emphasizes the importance of maintaining a solid reputation, not just in business, but in every facet of life. Buffett's belief is simple but profound:

"It takes 20 years to build a reputation and five minutes to ruin it."

Buffett's commitment to honesty and ethical behavior has been a cornerstone of his career. His transparency in dealings with business partners and investors has earned him trust and respect, both in the financial world and beyond. He stresses that no amount of financial gain is worth compromising your values or integrity.

Integrity in Business Decisions

One of the key moments where Buffett's reputation as a man of integrity stood out was during the **Salomon Brothers scandal** in the early 1990s. As the chairman of Salomon, Buffett was called in to manage the crisis when it was revealed that the company had engaged in illegal trading activities.

Instead of distancing himself or avoiding responsibility, Buffett took full accountability for the actions of the company. He didn't try to cover up the mistake or shift blame. Instead, he faced the public and promised to make the necessary changes to restore trust. His willingness to take responsibility earned him immense respect.

Trust as an Investment

Buffett also understands that **trust is invaluable**. When he talks about making investments, he often refers to the importance of the **people** behind a business. For him, the character of the people running a company is just as important as its financials. This principle is why he invests in companies with strong, ethical leadership.

For anyone looking to succeed in life, Buffett's wisdom here is essential: your reputation and trustworthiness will open doors that money can't. In business, in relationships, and in personal development, integrity is a foundation that supports long-term success.

Takeaway: Protect Your Reputation

As Buffett's actions demonstrate, your reputation is worth more than any financial gain. Make integrity a non-negotiable part of your personal and professional life. By doing so, you will build trust with others, which in turn will open opportunities and provide long-lasting success.

How to Think Like Warren Buffett

Perhaps one of the most powerful aspects of Warren Buffett's approach is his mindset. His way of thinking is rooted in clarity, simplicity, and **rational decision-making**. Buffett's ability to remove emotion from his investment decisions and think logically is one of the reasons he has succeeded for so long. But what exactly does it mean to "think like Warren Buffett"? Let's break it down.

1. Focus on What You Know

Buffett's famous mantra is:

"Never invest in a business you cannot understand."

This might sound simple, but it's a powerful principle that many investors ignore. Buffett's success is rooted in his **circle of competence**—he focuses only on industries and businesses that he understands thoroughly. This allows him to make informed, confident decisions rather than chasing speculative investments.

2. Think Independently

Buffett is known for his independent thinking. While most investors follow trends and the latest hot tips, Buffett follows his own research and **deep analysis**. He once advised:

"The best thing you can do is avoid the crowd."

This independence allows Buffett to take advantage of opportunities that others may overlook. For instance, when he invested in **Geico** in the 1970s, many thought it was a risky move. But Buffett understood the company's unique business model and the potential for growth.

3. Don't Follow Emotions

Buffett is perhaps most famous for his advice to be **fearful when others are greedy** and **greedy when others are fearful**. He remains calm and level-headed during market downturns, often seeing opportunities where others see panic. His rational approach prevents him from making emotional decisions, which is crucial when the market is volatile.

4. Make Decisions Based on Value, Not Price

One of the most critical elements of Buffett's thinking is his focus on value over price. For him, it's not about whether a stock is **cheap** or **expensive**, but whether the business has intrinsic value. He looks for companies that are selling at a discount to their true worth.

5. Stay Patient and Disciplined

Lastly, Buffett's mindset is rooted in **discipline**. He sticks to his principles and avoids being swayed by trends. Buffett is patient, but he also acts decisively when the time is right.

Takeaway: Apply Buffett's Mindset

Thinking like Buffett involves becoming disciplined, focusing on what you know, and staying calm and rational in the face of uncertainty. It's about making **informed**

decisions and trusting the process, even when others may not understand your approach.

Chapter 6:

Warren Buffett's Greatest Investments

Warren Buffett's journey as an investor is not just about the billions he's accumulated—it's also about the strategic thinking, insights, and lessons he's learned along the way. His portfolio is a roadmap of his investment philosophy, and it's filled with stories of triumph, mistakes, and valuable lessons that anyone can learn from. In this chapter, we'll look at some of **Buffett's most iconic investments** that changed everything, examine **why some investments fail**, and explore how you can **apply Buffett's strategies** to your own investment journey.

Iconic Investments That Changed Everything

Warren Buffett's investment success is legendary, and much of it can be attributed to his ability to recognize valuable companies that others overlooked. His long-term strategy of buying businesses with strong fundamentals has paid off enormously. Let's look at some of his most iconic investments that not only brought him great returns but also cemented his reputation as the world's greatest investor.

Coca-Cola: A Timeless Investment

One of Buffett's most celebrated investments was in **Coca-Cola**. In 1988, Buffett purchased **Coca-Cola** shares for $1.3 billion—an amount that seemed astronomical at the time. Yet, this decision would go on to become one of the most lucrative of his career.

What makes Coca-Cola such a brilliant investment? It's a brand with **global recognition**, unparalleled brand loyalty, and a product that's consumed across generations. Buffett was quick to see that Coca-Cola wasn't just a soft drink manufacturer; it was a **timeless**

brand with deep market penetration, consistent profits, and room for growth.

The return on his investment speaks for itself. Over time, Coca-Cola became one of Berkshire Hathaway's most valuable assets, contributing billions to the company's bottom line. Buffett's purchase of Coca-Cola embodies his focus on investing in businesses that are not only financially sound but have **long-term staying power.**

American Express: Building Wealth on Trust

Another iconic investment for Buffett was his purchase of **American Express** in the 1960s. At the time, American Express was facing a major crisis: a scandal involving a fraud at the company's vegetable oil division nearly caused the company to collapse. Many investors sold their shares in a panic, but Buffett saw an opportunity.

Buffett understood that American Express was more than just a credit card company—it was a brand that represented **trust**, **security**, and **prestige**. Despite the scandal, Buffett believed in the company's ability to recover, and his instincts were right. His early investment in American Express turned into one of Berkshire Hathaway's most profitable holdings.

Geico: Betting on the Underdog

In the 1970s, Buffett took a big risk by investing in **Geico**, an upstart insurance company that was struggling to compete with established firms. Despite skepticism from many of his peers, Buffett believed that Geico had a **unique business model** that could disrupt the industry.

Buffett was particularly drawn to Geico's direct-to-consumer model, which allowed it to offer lower prices than competitors. By analyzing the fundamentals, he saw the potential for Geico to scale up and dominate the market. Over time, Geico grew into one of Berkshire Hathaway's largest and most profitable investments, proving that Buffett's ability to see value when others didn't is a key part of his investment success.

Takeaway: Focus on the Fundamentals

Buffett's investments in Coca-Cola, American Express, and Geico have all followed a simple but powerful principle: **focus on businesses with strong fundamentals.** These companies offered great products, strong market positions, and clear paths to future growth. Buffett's willingness to invest in companies that were undervalued at the time, based on solid financial principles, is a strategy that anyone can apply.

Why Some Investments Fail

While Buffett's track record is stellar, no investor is without mistakes. Understanding why some of his investments didn't work out can teach us valuable lessons about risk management, decision-making, and how to avoid common pitfalls in investing.

The Berkshire Hathaway Purchase: A Lesson in Overconfidence

The story of Buffett's purchase of **Berkshire Hathaway** itself is an example of how even Buffett can make mistakes. Buffett originally bought Berkshire Hathaway in the 1960s when it was a struggling textile company. At the time, he thought he could turn the company around. However, the textile business was in decline, and Buffett soon realized that the investment would never be the cash cow he had hoped for.

Rather than cutting his losses early, Buffett continued to invest in Berkshire, turning it into a holding company that acquired other businesses. Despite the fact that the initial purchase was a **mistake**, Buffett's eventual transformation of the company into the powerhouse conglomerate it is today shows how a bad decision can sometimes be turned around with **adaptability** and **strategic thinking**.

Dexter Shoe: A Costly Mistake

Another of Buffett's famous mistakes was his investment in **Dexter Shoe Company** in 1993. Buffett bought the company for $433 million in stock. However, Dexter Shoes struggled against cheaper competitors, and its value quickly declined. In hindsight, Buffett admitted that the investment was a mistake, particularly because Berkshire paid for Dexter with **Berkshire stock**, meaning that the value of the purchase actually cost much more than it was worth.

The Dexter Shoe debacle highlights the importance of thoroughly understanding the business dynamics of any company before making an investment. Despite this setback, Buffett still preaches that even the best investors make mistakes, and the key is to **learn from them** and move on.

Takeaway: Learn from Mistakes

Even Buffett acknowledges that mistakes are a part of investing. The important lesson here is to recognize when an investment isn't working, **cut your losses** early, and **move forward**.

Mistakes are inevitable, but how you respond to them will determine your long-term success.

What You Can Learn from Buffett's Portfolio

Buffett's portfolio is a treasure trove of investment lessons. By studying his approach, investors can glean important insights into how to think about value, risk, and the market. Here are some of the key lessons that you can apply to your own investing strategy.

The Importance of Patience

One of the key takeaways from Buffett's portfolio is the importance of **long-term thinking**. Most of Buffett's best investments—like Coca-Cola, American Express, and Geico—were not profitable overnight. They required patience, discipline, and time to realize their full potential. This reinforces Buffett's mantra:

"Our favorite holding period is forever."

As an individual investor, it's tempting to chase quick returns, especially in volatile markets. However, Buffett's track record teaches us that the best results come from investing in solid companies with long-term potential and holding onto them for years—sometimes even decades.

Invest in What You Understand

Buffett's investment strategy is rooted in the idea that you should only invest in companies and industries that you understand. By keeping within your **circle of competence**, you can make smarter, more confident decisions. Buffett avoided the dot-com boom and other speculative bubbles because he didn't fully understand those businesses. For individual investors, this is crucial advice: stick to industries and businesses where you have **knowledge** or can easily **understand the basics**.

Look for Value, Not Hype

Buffett has made a career of investing in companies that are **undervalued**, not ones driven by hype. In fact, he famously avoided the **dot-com** boom in the late 1990s, recognizing that the valuations of many tech stocks were not based on solid fundamentals. Instead, Buffett invested in companies with **steady earnings**, strong management, and proven track records.

For the average investor, Buffett's approach is a reminder to **look beyond the market hype** and focus on the true value of a business.

Takeaway: Adopt Buffett's Investment Philosophy

The core of Buffett's strategy is simple but powerful: invest in companies with strong fundamentals, understand the businesses you're investing in, and have the patience to wait for those investments to grow. If you approach investing with a clear, disciplined strategy like Buffett's, you'll be well-positioned for long-term succe

Chapter 7:
Buffett the Teacher – Lessons for Life and Business

Warren Buffett is not just an extraordinary investor; he is also a teacher who generously shares his wisdom. His investment strategies, philosophies, and principles are valuable lessons for anyone who wants to succeed—not only in investing but also in business and life. In this chapter, we will explore some of Buffett's most significant teachings and how you can apply them to your own journey. Whether you're an aspiring investor, entrepreneur, or just someone looking to improve your financial habits, the **lessons from the Oracle of Omaha** are timeless.

How to Build a Personal Investing Strategy

One of the most powerful aspects of Buffett's investment approach is his ability to keep things simple. He doesn't chase trends or try to time the market; instead, he follows a disciplined approach based on clear principles. For those looking to create their own personal investing strategy, Buffett's lessons can be incredibly useful.

Start Small and Be Patient

Buffett's first piece of advice to any new investor is to start small and gradually build your portfolio over time. He famously says, "The stock market is a device for transferring money from the impatient to the patient." It's easy to get caught up in the excitement of trying to make quick gains, but Buffett teaches that the real rewards come to those who can practice patience.

For beginners, this means starting with manageable amounts of money that you're willing to commit for the long term. Instead of chasing every hot stock or speculative trend,

Buffett suggests investing in companies that you understand well and that have a clear path to long-term growth.

Create Your Circle of Competence

One of Buffett's key teachings is to **invest within your circle of competence**—that is, to invest in businesses that you fully understand. He often advises that the best investments are the ones that **make sense to you,** not the ones that everyone else is talking about. By focusing on industries, products, and companies that you are knowledgeable about, you can make more informed decisions and feel confident in your investments.

For example, if you understand the fundamentals of the food and beverage industry, you may consider investing in companies like **Coca-Cola**. If you have a passion for technology, look for tech companies that show strong potential and make sure you understand the business models behind them.

Keep It Simple and Avoid Complexity

Buffett has always championed simplicity in investing. He avoids complex, speculative investments and instead focuses on simple, well-established businesses with strong financials. He famously stated, "Never invest in a business you cannot understand."

This lesson is important for investors at all levels. Too often, people are tempted by **complex financial products** or **short-term market swings**, but Buffett's strategy is built on **understanding** and **clarity**. By sticking to investments that are straightforward and easy to grasp, you reduce the risk of making costly mistakes.

Takeaway: Build Your Strategy with Patience and Simplicity

The key takeaway here is that a personal investing strategy should be built on patience, knowledge, and simplicity. Buffett encourages new investors to take the time to learn and to focus on investments they understand, while also practicing patience and resisting the urge for instant gratification.

Living Below Your Means

Despite being one of the wealthiest individuals in the world, Warren Buffett lives a remarkably **frugal** lifestyle. His personal approach to money is grounded in **financial discipline** and the belief that true wealth comes from managing your expenses, not simply earning more money.

Frugality and Financial Discipline

Buffett has always adhered to the principle of **living below your means**. He famously still resides in the modest house he bought in 1958 for $31,500, even though his net worth is in the billions. He drives an old car, enjoys simple pleasures like playing bridge, and prioritizes **saving and investing** over spending.

Buffett's lifestyle teaches us that the key to financial success isn't necessarily about earning a high income; it's about how much you **save** and how wisely you manage your spending. Living below your means doesn't mean depriving yourself—it means being **disciplined** with your spending and investing the difference.

The Importance of Financial Independence

Buffett has often said that the secret to a happy life is **financial independence**. This means having enough money to live comfortably without worrying about bills or making ends meet. But the true benefit of financial independence, according to Buffett, is that it allows you to live your life on your own terms.

By spending wisely and saving consistently, you can gradually build wealth without the constant pressure to work harder or make more money. The goal isn't just about accumulating riches—it's about **gaining freedom** and being able to make choices that align with your values and priorities.

Takeaway: Focus on Saving and Financial Discipline

Buffett's frugality teaches an important lesson: financial success is not determined by how much money you make, but by how much you save and invest. The key to long-term financial health is **living within your means**, saving regularly, and investing wisely.

Balancing Wealth and Generosity

In addition to his impressive business acumen, Warren Buffett is known for his **philanthropy**. Buffett's approach to wealth isn't just about accumulating money for personal gain; it's about **using wealth to make a positive impact** in the world. Through his commitment to philanthropy, Buffett has shown that **generosity** is just as important as financial success.

The Giving Pledge

In 2010, Buffett and Bill Gates launched the **Giving Pledge**, a commitment by the world's wealthiest individuals to give away the majority of their wealth to charitable causes. Buffett himself has pledged to give away **99% of his wealth** over his lifetime, with most of it going to the Bill and Melinda Gates Foundation, which focuses on global health and poverty alleviation.

Buffett's philanthropic efforts teach an important lesson: true wealth isn't measured by how much you accumulate, but by the positive impact you have on others. Giving generously allows you to leave a lasting legacy that goes beyond your personal success.

Wealth and Responsibility

Buffett believes that with great wealth comes great responsibility. He frequently talks about the privilege of being able to help others and the importance of using wealth for **good**. His view is that wealth should be used to **improve the**

lives of others and contribute to causes that are important to you.

By emphasizing the idea of **responsible wealth**, Buffett teaches that **generosity** isn't just about writing a check—it's about using your resources, time, and talents to **create lasting change** in the world.

Takeaway: Wealth Should Be Used for Good

The final lesson from Buffett's life is that wealth isn't just for personal enjoyment; it's meant to be used to **make the world a better place**. His **Giving Pledge** serves as a powerful reminder that once you reach a certain level of financial success, you have a responsibility to give back and contribute to the greater good.

Chapter 9:
The Legacy of Warren Buffett – The Billionaire Who Inspired the World

Warren Buffett's name is synonymous with investing wisdom, financial success, and philanthropy. However, his legacy extends far beyond his accomplishments in the stock market. Over the years, Buffett has built a reputation not only as a brilliant investor but also as a **humble, ethical leader** who has profoundly influenced the world. His strategies, principles, and personal philosophy have shaped the investing world and continue to inspire millions of people worldwide. In this chapter, we'll explore how Buffett's legacy has impacted both the financial world and the lives of those he's mentored, and provide you with actionable takeaways to carry his wisdom into your own life.

A Timeless Impact on Investing

Warren Buffett's **value investing** philosophy has left a lasting mark on the world of finance. When he began his investment journey, the landscape was dominated by speculative, short-term traders who sought to capitalize on market fluctuations. Buffett's approach was different—he focused on **buying quality companies** at a fair price and holding them for the long term. This strategy was grounded in **fundamental analysis**, **business models**, and the belief in **intrinsic value**.

The Revolution of Value Investing

Buffett was introduced to value investing by his mentor, Benjamin Graham, whose book *The Intelligent Investor* was foundational to Buffett's early career. However, Buffett did not merely follow Graham's teachings; he **evolved** them.

Graham's philosophy focused on finding "cigar-butt" stocks—companies that were undervalued but had little future potential. Buffett, on the other hand, sought out **wonderful businesses** at reasonable prices—companies with sustainable competitive advantages, solid management teams, and a proven track record.

Through his investments in companies like **Coca-Cola, American Express**, and **Geico**, Buffett demonstrated how long-term value investing could yield substantial returns. His strategy encouraged investors to take a patient, disciplined approach and focus on **fundamentals** rather than market speculation.

As a result, Buffett's influence revolutionized the investment world, and his approach became a blueprint for many investors, both institutional and individual. His success has also inspired a **new generation** of value investors who now view **stock market investing** as a long-term pursuit of financial freedom rather than a quick path to wealth.

Buffett's Influence on the Investing World

Buffett's impact on the investing world goes beyond the companies he's invested in and the wealth he's accumulated. He has created a movement—a **philosophy of patience**, **integrity**, and **prudence** that values intelligent investing over flashy trends. His emphasis on **long-term thinking** has influenced countless investors, helping them avoid the pitfalls of **short-term speculation** and instead focus on investing in companies with strong fundamentals.

Buffett's influence is also reflected in the **Buffett Rule**, which calls for fair taxation of the wealthy and greater financial transparency. Through his own **financial success**, Buffett has shown that it is possible to achieve great wealth by doing the right thing, both ethically and financially. In turn, his teachings have helped democratize **investment knowledge**, encouraging individuals from all walks of life to take charge of their financial futures.

The Human Side of Warren Buffett

While Warren Buffett's financial genius is what most people know him for, his personal character and values are just as remarkable. He is not only a brilliant investor but also a **humble human being** who has built lifelong relationships based on trust, generosity, and integrity. Buffett's approach to life—his values, his relationships, and his leadership style—adds another layer to his legacy, making him a role model for aspiring entrepreneurs, business leaders, and investors.

Humility and Personal Relationships

Despite his immense wealth and global fame, Buffett remains remarkably humble. He is often described as down-to-earth, approachable, and grounded in his values. His humility is best illustrated by his simple lifestyle. Buffett has lived in the same house in Omaha, Nebraska, since 1958, and he continues to drive modest cars and lead a lifestyle that focuses more on **family, friends,** and **intellectual pursuits** than on material luxury.

Buffett's relationships with his family, friends, and colleagues demonstrate his deep belief in the importance of trust and integrity. He has always been known to treat people with kindness and respect, and his leadership at **Berkshire Hathaway** reflects a belief in treating employees with fairness and generosity. Buffett has often said that he values **loyalty** above all else, and this trait has earned him the admiration of his peers and employees alike.

Moreover, Buffett has mentored countless individuals over the years. His partnership with **Charlie Munger**, his right-hand man at Berkshire Hathaway, is one of the most famous and successful business relationships in history. Buffett has always been open to sharing his knowledge and providing advice, and many of his mentees attribute their success to his guidance and mentorship.

Buffett as a Teacher

As much as Buffett is known for his investment prowess, he is equally revered as a teacher. He has spent decades giving speeches, writing letters, and holding shareholder meetings in which he shares his investment philosophy, his lessons learned, and his insights on life. In fact, many of his most influential teachings have come through his annual **Berkshire Hathaway shareholder letters**, which have become a sort of guidebook for investors.

Buffett's ability to break down complex financial concepts into simple, digestible lessons has made him a beloved teacher. He teaches not only about investing but about the importance of **character, integrity**, and **patience**. His ability to simplify abstract concepts and relate them to real-world experiences has made him an icon of both the investing world and the broader business community.

Carrying Buffett's Wisdom into the Future

As Warren Buffett approaches the later years of his life, his legacy will undoubtedly continue to inspire generations of investors, business leaders, and individuals seeking to live a life of purpose. While Buffett's direct influence may one day wane, the lessons he has imparted will live on, providing timeless wisdom for future generations.

Actionable Takeaways from Buffett's Legacy

So, how can you carry Warren Buffett's wisdom into your own life? Whether you're a beginner investor, an experienced entrepreneur, or simply someone looking to **improve their financial situation**, the teachings of the Oracle of Omaha can provide a blueprint for success.

Here are a few key takeaways from Buffett's life and legacy:

1. **Patience Pays Off**: Buffett's strategy of buying quality companies and holding

them for the long term is a powerful reminder that **wealth-building** takes time. Avoid the temptation to chase quick gains and instead focus on investments that offer long-term potential.

2. **Invest in What You Know**: Buffett's success is based on his deep understanding of the companies he invests in. By building a **circle of competence**, you can make smarter investment decisions and avoid making mistakes based on hype or speculation.

3. **Live with Integrity**: Buffett's emphasis on honesty, trust, and **integrity** has earned him the respect of the business world. In business and life, your reputation is invaluable. Always act with integrity and treat people with respect.

4. **Financial Independence is Key**: Through his frugal lifestyle and disciplined approach to money, Buffett

has shown that financial freedom comes not from earning a high income but from managing your money wisely. Live below your means, save consistently, and invest for the future.

5. **Give Back**: Buffett's commitment to philanthropy and his belief in using wealth for good is a vital part of his legacy. As you build your wealth, remember that true success isn't measured by what you accumulate but by the positive impact you make on the world.

Buffett's Wisdom in Action

The key to carrying Buffett's wisdom into the future is to incorporate his teachings into your **daily habits** and **financial decisions**. Whether it's taking a long-term approach to investing, building meaningful relationships based on trust, or living a life of integrity and generosity, you can create a legacy of your own by applying the principles that have made Buffett one of the world's most respected figures.

www.ingramcontent.com/pod-product-compliance
Lightning Source LLC
Chambersburg PA
CBHW050326230526
45471CB00005B/2370